Telling My Father

JAMES CREWS

Telling My Father

JAMES CREWS

SOUTHEAST MISSOURI STATE UNIVERSITY PRESS
2017

Telling My Father
By James Crews

Copyright 2017 James Crews

ISBN: 978-0-9979262-5-5
Softcover: $15.00

First published in 2017 by
Southeast Missouri State University Press
One University Plaza, MS 2650
Cape Girardeau, MO 63701
www.semopress.com

Cover Design: Carrie Walker

Table of Contents

Part IV

for my father, James H. Crews, Sr. (1957–2000)

Human Being

The human part of us
wants and needs and breaks,
but the being part sees
beyond the body's aching
joints and joyful noises
to the open road ahead.
The gravel is covered
in a fine layer of snow
and ice with the white sun
shining through a tunnel
of pines like the unblinking
eye of the source.

The human part of us
knows that if we keep going
we will slip and slide
and fall down endlessly,
but the being part says
so what? and pushes us
onward toward the light,
since it knows there is
no way but to move
forward, step by step
in our heavy boots.

Chore

Too young to help, I watched my father
hack and dig at the old oak stump,
pulling up taproots whose prickly hairs
clung to bits of red clay they brought
into lake-chilled air. He chipped away
at heartwood gone soft in rain until
it became a pile of pulp around a hole
in the ground filled with soil and seed.
Smelling of sweat and tobacco now,
he took off his T-shirt, wiped his face.
We worked hard today, didn't we, he said.
I think we deserve a little rest. And I nodded.
We lay back among clumps of grass
as dusk spread across the field and a fine
mist fell over us like a net, pressing
our bodies to the steaming earth.

My Father Asks for One Last Thing

Bending over rows of four o'clocks
now wet with evening, he picks off
dead blooms, tipping their seeds
into an envelope for next year,
though he knows he won't be here.
Through the screen door, I smell
cut grass, wild onion, gasoline.
Under his T-shirt stained green,
his skin's already begun to yellow
like a window shade finally ruined
by too much smoke and sun.
Gloaming is not the word for how
night shows up, draping the city sky
whose trapped sulfur and junk-light
fight off true dark. He looks up
from cleaning the mower blades,
knows I'm checking on him again.
I open the pantry, pretend to be
absorbed by the jars of tomatoes
he canned last summer, heirlooms
floating soft in the murk of time.
And when he calls my name, asking
for a massage, having asked too much
of his body today, his face is blank
and gray like the sky before rain.

Halfway-Heaven

Before he died, my father tried to teach me
the only language of manhood he knew—
Phillips head, needle-nose, catalytic converter—
but I left him hunched under hoods
or sprawled on cardboard pallets beneath
stalled cars, thinking the dust of books
and the green glow of computer screens
could keep me from work like that. I hated
his oil-stink, the orange goop he used
to clean his grease-black hands, and those
homemade tattoos of lightning on his biceps.
I hated the cigarette dangling from his lips,
his eyes squinting against smoke snaking up
as he scraped a deer skull clean of meat
for mounting. But now, I want it all back.
I replay every scene in my mind as if
seeing my father again could keep him alive
and tinkering in some other realm, some
halfway-heaven he'd love because everything
needs fixing there. I think of the green-
striped tube socks pulled to his knees when he
mowed the yard, the scratch of sandpaper-
stubble against my cheek each time he
kissed me goodnight. I still hear the way
he'd say *sorta speak* when he meant *so to speak,*
while explaining, for instance, why tomatoes
taste better with a kiss of salt: *Brings out
the sweetness, sorta speak.*

Strict Diet

Though the doctors said no salt,
salt was all my father craved.
His body bloated, skin water-logged
and gray, still he wanted potato chips,
honey-baked ham, greasy slabs
of Polish sausage from Piekutowski's.
He begged for pepperoni pizza,
garlic butter, ribs slathered in sauce.
But when I did the shopping,
I searched only for labels that said
low sodium and *no preservatives*, instead
bringing home heads of broccoli,
turkey burgers, shredded wheat.
And when he died anyway,
guilt gnawed me like an ulcer—
how could I have denied him
his few final pleasures?—
until I found Big Mac wrappers
stuffed under the car seat,
jars of pickles in the hall closet,
and hidden among wads of tissues
near the night stand, his stash—
a half-used canister of salt.
I sat down on his sagging mattress
now stripped of stained sheets
and studied that blue label
with the girl in the yellow dress
holding her umbrella against a rain
of salt still falling from the sky.

In the Yard After a Storm

I placed the acorn cap in my palm
like the smallest alms bowl, held it up
to catch the last drops of rain falling
cold from the tips of shivering leaves.
But as I turned it over, let the water
trickle out, it became the polished knob
to a trapdoor that appears only for those
who wait long enough to see its shadow
hung on mist and air. I pulled, lifted,
then looked down as if into that place
carved out in my mind like a cellar filled
with the murky jars of my worst fears,
their labels faded but the message clear:
To know myself, I must taste each one.

In the Middle of the Night

I'm up again because I have dreamed
my father alive, rustling rubber sheets
to get my attention and lying there
in the spare room as he did at the end
surrounded by the stares of mounted
game—elk, deer and bobcat hung
on the walls around the foldout couch.

But he was young and thin in my dream,
the tattoos that shamed him flashing on
sculpted biceps, his hair that had turned
white too soon gone back to brown.
And as usual in the dream, he refused
to speak to me, his mouth moving,
teeth gnashing some phantom-sound
that would not come out as words.

In this sleepless house is the ticking
sound I call *settling* to steady my mind.
The dark outside is taking its time
lifting its stain from the skin of snow
by slow degrees. Do I call him forth
out of ether? Ask him why he can't
talk back? I fill another kettle, place it
on the flames. And listen. And wait.

The Inheritance

Digging through a box of my father's things,
beneath cracked eyeglasses and jars of nails,
I find the rusted but still sharp switchblade
his old man had given him. I let the bone handle
take me back to that distant St. Louis night
when my father and his buddy, fresh from a shift
at Grossman Steel, passed a pint of Jim Beam
back and forth and tore along Kingshighway
to the park where men went for other men.
Bodies flashed past as they eased among oaks
and grassy hillsides studded with used rubbers.
As catcalls began to reach their slowing car,
a man approached, some ghost in skin-tight Levi's
leaning close with his *Hey baby*, running a finger
along my father's arm and tracing the new tattoo—
a bolt of black lightning on his tightening biceps.
The knife snapped open quick, and my father
stabbed the air near the man's face until he turned
and sprinted. Gunning the engine, they chased
that pale figure zigzagging like a spooked rabbit
until he fell to the asphalt, then into a ravine—
my father still laughing, still stabbing the night air
with the knife I now hold.

Elegy for Faces Nightclub, East St. Louis

I parked the car and crossed the gravel lot strewn
with used condoms and needles, then handed

my five to the bouncer, who glanced at my fake ID
and with a yawn waved me inside my first gay bar.

The music was turned low, no bass, nothing but
Madonna and a single soul stirring on the dance floor.

Balding men lingered on stools, tapping their sneakers
to "Lucky Star"—*I just think of you and I start to glow*—

as they stroked the necks of Bud Lights. Even below,
in the basement where a sign proclaimed, *Men Only*,

I found it mostly deserted, TVs bolted to the ceiling
flickering the flesh of outdated and grainy porn

outside unused rooms set aside for those who liked it
quick and anonymous. For the rest of the night,

I inhaled smoke, downed Jell-O shots, climbed inside
empty cages. But when the crowd got thicker, I struck up

a dance with a wisp-thin boy from Elgin, Illinois,
and we moved in sync under spinning rainbow strobes,

music pounding in our chests—yet I kept my distance,
even as his eyes roved the folds of my too-tight jeans,

even when he put his mouth near my ear and whispered,
Take me home—a plea no man had ever made to me.

I can't help but regret how I pulled away, told him no,
made him scrawl a phone number I would never call

on my sweaty palm as I kissed his cheek goodbye
under a cloudless daybreak sky going slowly pink.

Telling My Father

I found him on the porch that morning,
sipping cold coffee, watching a crow
dip down from the power line into the pile
of black bags stuffed in the dumpster
where he pecked and snagged a can tab,
then carried it off, clamped in his beak
like the key to a room only he knew about.
My father turned to me then, taking in
the reek of my smoke, traces of last night's
eyeliner I decided not to wipe off this time.
Out late was all he said. And then smiled,
rubbing the small of my back through the robe
for a while, before heading inside, letting
the storm door click shut behind him.
Later, when I stepped into the kitchen,
I saw it waiting there on the table—a glass
of orange juice he had poured for me and left
sweating in a patch of sunlight so bright
I couldn't touch it at first.

While You Were Sleeping

The light, always too bright this early,
has a vibratory quality as it shines
through the box fan propped
in the window, the blades spinning
and pulling inside the only cool air
we'll feel today. Inside, it's calm:
the carpet soaks up the slight sound
of our breathing, the creaking of joints
as I stretch my legs and fill the time
before you wake with plans and lists.
The wide green leaves of the fig tree
outside the window are already lit
and spread like hands to grip the sun
that also swells the bulbs of fruit
hanging from each tangled branch.
In bed, you turn and sigh, dragging
the duvet back over your head.
I'm the one who most often rises
when daylight floods the one room
of our tiny house, pushing through
the picture windows in front of which
we've strung strips of rope with chimes
to keep the birds from careening
into the blue sky and tree they see
reflected in the glass, to keep us
from having to hear the soft thud
of another stunned hummingbird
falling to the front porch. The ropes
obstruct the view, but I don't mind
as long as I can still look out and see
the ancient ash tree whose crown
is wider than this house, whose branches
could cradle the whole place if some
unlikely cyclone should ever lift us
from the foundation and toss us

among the wind-trembled leaves.
This is the only quiet time I have,
a half hour to forty-five minutes
before the city sounds combine with
the relentless electric sun to keep me
from privacy. I need this natural silence
before leaf-blowers, weed-eaters,
and trash trucks claim the neighborhood,
before the chorus of dogs takes up
yipping and howling. I sit here, grateful
for the breeze filtering through
fig leaves wet from last night's rain
as you turn over, wide awake now,
and say, *Come back to me.* I do.

First Kiss

Imagine that first accidental
brushing of mouths between
two men in a fire-lit cave,
how they pulled away and vowed
it would never happen again,
though the pleasure receptors
embedded in their lips said
differently. And when they met
once more, this time on a trail
in the woods, they couldn't resist:
they brought their mouths
together, kissing over and over—
one man having freshened
his breath with mint, the other
having rubbed beeswax
across his lips to make them
even sweeter.

Waiting for Love

You must save up for it and collect and gather honey.
—Rainer Maria Rilke

You can collect as much of it as you like,
keep it in trunks under the bed, in closets
or store it in stone jars as the pharaohs did,
placing gallon after gallon of priceless honey
next to the alabaster heads of sarcophagi
so when they woke wide-eyed and famished
in the afterlife, they'd find something familiar
and sweet to eat. But nothing hoarded stays
hidden for long. Soon enough some looter
will shimmy into that secret room in you and—
ignoring the warnings—pry off the lid
of every jar and scoop out what is now
crystallized, shining in his hands, somehow
still delicious after all that time.

What Goes On

The flame's the same in each of us
though it is not eternal
just as I am not eternal
no matter how permanent I feel
when lying next to my lover
and leaning close before bed
to leave a kiss as a kind of seal
on his lips, to prove that we are real
and feel and fall and try to fit
ourselves imperfectly back together.
But if in the night one of us
should wake with the taste of ash
in his mouth, afraid of how fast
all of this might end, the walls
of the mind closing in, and the soul
flying up in a wisp of smoke
to join the sky again—
then let us rest a palm against
the sleeping chest of the other
and understand that muted drumbeat
as the song of every warm body
happy to be alive in the universe.
Let that music remind us
no part of us was meant to last
except for the heat we gave
in the form of a love that goes on
long after we're gone.

After Love

Something startles me where I thought I was safest.
—Walt Whitman

While you slept, one arm pinning me
against the bed, I watched a pigeon limp
across the skylight, his tiny feet printing
a message in soot and dust I took to mean:
Suffer the limits and learn to praise this dream.
But I could not stand the way pleasure
clouds the mind, turns words to moans
in a pillow, stones in the throat, then leaves
on the wind of each breath after, lifting
from us through the pores of skin bent
on feeling more, again, soon. The pigeon
flapped his wings, that simple, and rose up
into the fog now rolling across the bay,
pushing through the window I'd left open,
hoping for some sun and not the flies
that lit on our bodies—buzzing, feasting,
having their way with us.

God Bud

He took the glass pipe from his lips,
his face lost for a moment in the smudge
of smoke that clung to the air as he exhaled.
When it cleared, I could see he'd slipped
beneath the surface of himself, a stone
dropped in the pond of each green eye
as he knelt on the floor before me as if
for worship, and packed the last of his stash
into the pipe's bowl, telling me
it was my turn to try this strain of weed
called *god bud* for the way it cuts a path
through the mind's clutter to the place
where revelation is supposed to take root.
I have never believed that pleasure
outranks pain, that beauty trumps truth,
but I let him press the tip of that warm pipe
to my lips, his lighter-flame licking
the purplish leaves awake as I sucked in
the smoke, holding it so long my lungs ached,
and my eyes began to water—when God
enters me, I thought, I want it to burn.

God Spot

God would never speak to us in tongues
or show his face in patches of shower mold,
on burnt toast or a steamed-up window
when he could just touch that place
in the brain said to be the sole sweet spot
where we link with his signals.

Maybe it's those beams we're searching for
when our dreaming eyes blink wild
behind our shut-tight lids, scanning
scenes that stream from the sky
for a sign of the ghost-light that makes
each mind a homing device.

Last night, when I felt the sudden weight
of someone sitting on the edge of my bed,
I shot up in the dark and pressed a hand
to my chest. *Are you there?* I almost asked,
but the question faded as my eyes
adjusted to the earthly shadows

of dresser, nightstand, and armchair
in the empty room. I got up and stood
in the square of streetlight shining
like a door on the floor, and I listened
as my heart hammered home its lone
message: *I'm here, I'm here, I'm here.*

God Particles

I could almost hear their soft collisions
on the cold air today, but when I came in,

shed my layers and stood alone by the fire,
I felt them float toward me like spores

flung far from their source, having crossed
miles of oceans and fields unknown to most

just to keep my body fixed to its place
on the earth. Call them *God* if you must,

these messengers that bring hard evidence
of what I once was and where I have been—

filling me with bits of stardust, whaleskin,
goosedown from the pillow where Einstein

slept, tucked in his cottage in New Jersey,
dreaming of things I know I'll never see.

Salmon River Estuary, First Light

When the animals went ashore to take up life on
land, they carried part of the sea in their bodies.
—Rachel Carson

On the beach where I stand,
retreating water has left its mark,
having etched a set of ripples
in the slick sand that would shine
in silvering moonlight if the moon
were not a closed eye behind a lid
of cloud, if I could see through
the bruise of overcast sky and know
what waits on the other side.
I've heard of bobcat and cougar here,
but no steps rustle in the understory
of firs at my back. The only sound
is the crush of the surf beckoning me
over and over with the voice
and rhythm of my own heartbeat,
salt calling to the salt in the blood
that washes through us all.

Mad River, Mid-Morning

When the salted wind picks up,
gnats hover on the air until it seems
the slightest breath will send them
onward, and it does. I used to wonder
why these curlews, plovers and gulls
act so hungry here, but you would say
that's just how they see the world:
each millet seed or piece of bread
a single note in some future song.
I remember that winter in Chicago
when we woke in your blue room
above the bakery and smoked all day,
steaming the windows, eating scones
as hard as stones while the el train
shook the mattress we scarcely left.
Love, which is not the same as God,
floats like the bottle on the current,
filling, emptying, as if on command.
This egret and the mist can teach us
the delicacy with which they lift
from the spit, testing the waters
farther out, skimming those deep
dark places we can never reach.

When I Think of the End of the World

I can't help but see the crocuses
that will somehow push through
layers of ash like tender fingers
still green enough to redeem
the particulate drizzle that will
keep staining our expectant faces
as we huddle in cellars or crouch
under overpasses on hazmat pallets
wondering how to fill the silence
piling above us like snow.

I see Pavlov, gaunt and sweating
on his deathbed, requesting only
a bowl of mud from the creek
near his boyhood home in Ryazan
where he once sailed paper boats
and packed pies so thick his mouth
would water. When he cradled
that dish of earth, he must have
sighed, smiling, sinking both hands
deep into memory so his fever
had no choice but to break.

I think of you and hear the train
sparking to a stop beneath your room
on Killingsworth Street, that voice
warning the tired passengers slowly
pouring out into the night: *Doors
are closing.* I wish I could go back now
and tape those sounds you made
when we made love, though I know,
or say I know, there is no way
to replay them.

As You Label It, So It Appears to You

If I say I see a heron lifting off
hours before dawn, I mean I see
a long, blue piece of me unraveling
from the dark, landing in the creek
to hunt a glint of fish, then taking it
writhing into a mouth silvered by
light some call the moon, but which
is only a buffed steel cap that barely
holds back the spill of summer sun.
The heron can already sense the water
warming up the way we know a word
spoken to a glass of liquid over time
will change its molecules: Call it *holy*,
holy is what you will taste.

Midnight Snow

Outside in the creek that feeds the lake
and never freezes, an otter slaps the water
with his paw to feel the current's pulse
which tells him to slip and lie back.
He shuts his eyes and obeys, knowing
the layers of hair and underfur will keep
warming him while he floats on a faith
we wish could carry us the same.

The sound of his splashing soon fades,
but not his joy in being pushed, as light
as driftwood, back to the mouth of the den
I've seen carved out in the roots of a fir
now packed with snow and lined with leaves
that promise his sleep will be deep.

Because no dreams wait softly for me,
I open the woodstove and strike a match.
I hold the bloom of flame to kindling
and make my wish: To be that slick body
sliding into the lake without so much
as a shiver, no doubt about where
I'm going or how to get there.

Crater Lake

I dip the Mason jar into the melting lake
and the water rushes in sweet as a medicine
I have somehow lived without until tonight.
In the half-dark, in the fever of a wolf moon,
I move closer to the rim where the walls
of this caldera still recall the heat and flow
of the volcano it once was, where the rock
remembers the hands that gripped it, the feet
that kicked against it to give the swimmer
momentum. This lake knows the strokes
of every fish-fin, the glance and swoop
of the heron, the knock of our earthly oars—
our voices—but there are still some secrets
it must keep. Capping my jar, I hold it
up to the stars and let the water store
the unstrung rosary of those worn lights.
I drink, and then I see the native seekers
who once came here to swim day and night,
opening their eyes underwater to catch
the spirits in the act of making that blue
world shimmer. And after they had touched
the source of ecstasy and pain—that single
place in each of us—they would rise slowly
to the surface and climb out of the lake,
now shamans. For hours, they would spurn
all fire, shrugging off elk-skins, leaving
their skin bare to the howling white wind.

Becoming the Wolf

Drinking from the creek after his meal
scavenged from one of the frozen elk,
the wolf knows the body tells two stories—
I want, I need—and ponders the difference
as he stalks back to his den, where his throat
will throb with a long song sent to the sky
to say, *You are not so alone you cannot be saved.*
Tonight, the wind is a dull knife crying
for the whetstone, prying at the windows.
Icicles, like flutes, slip from the eaves
and carve their own throats in snow—
thin hollows the clouds will fill before
a voice can take hold. I cannot sing
to the moon using notes it knows, or look
with eyes that catch the right light to hunt by.
So I must huddle in this blanket-cave,
scraps of stringy words stuck in my teeth—
cold flesh that must be ripped bit by bit
from the ribs of helpless things.

For Those Weary of Prayer

Surely you know that time of night
when fireflies, tired of their own SOS,
float right into the mouth of a net,
when cicadas begin to sense they are
nothing more than husks for the chorus
that fills them. Surely you have seen
a child slough his trunks and run naked
through a sprinkler, crying out with joy
as you call him to bed. Aren't you always
calling the name of what you love most
back to you, over and over, holding
the door open and pleading, *Please don't
make me ask again*—and then asking again
until he comes?

How Light Leaves

Light leaves this summer day
the way it leaves the eyes,

not all at once, but by slow degrees,
reaching through the blinds,

touching the tabletop and turning
the glass of water into fuel,

making it burn before dropping
behind poplars and glancing

one last time through leaves
now shimmering, flickering out.

The light left my father's eyes
like that, until his look became

a darkened glass behind which
I knew he was still awake,

but lying alone now, waiting
for a knock at the door, and then

the light footsteps of someone
coming for him.

Last Kiss

I wondered if anybody would ever love me that much
when I walked into the hospital room and saw my mother
gripping the metal bedrails, eyes ravaged as she smoothed
the gray hair from my father's forehead. He was dead,

lips parted a little as if he'd been taken in mid-breath
or was about to call out the name of something on the tip
of his tongue. When he died, I was at a diner eating
French fries with my lover, who was already in love

with someone else. There were so many people in the room,
but I remember only my mother in the plastic chair
unable to leave him. *Come here*, she said, *and kiss your father
goodbye.* But I couldn't move. I watched the snow falling

outside his window, heard the distant chopping propellers
of a helicopter I imagined bearing a cooler-full of organs
other patients were waiting for. My mother waved me over,
and I knew then I couldn't refuse, though I also knew

my father no longer filled the stiffening body she caressed.
I kissed the creases of his cold forehead, then pulled away
as fast as I could, taking with me the last of his breath.

First Breath

Something blows a gust of wind into us
when we are born, and a flame leaps up
in our chest: The lamp at last is lit.
We cry out, the heat's too much. We take
our first breaths, and the fire flares,
growing brighter as the light of the white
room into which we've been ushered
sears our eyes like a revelation we will
always be trying to decipher. Is this
the first moment we meet God without
a single word to name him? Everything
trembles and waits for our attention
so that we might recognize the force that
courses through us as the same that moves
through the tree, the dog, even the bars
of the crib where we first sleep.
When does it happen that we understand
we must now guard the flame as our own,
must find ways to feed it and keep it
from going out? Sometimes I don't want
to love because every instance of reaching
for another takes me back to that time
of tiny hands clawing at the empty air,
my body exposed, every sound I made
refusing to shape itself into a language
for want, for need. Even now, when a cold
wind blows against me, my gloved hand
hangs at my side, waiting to be held,
reassured, and a sharp pang passes
through me as I remember the warmth
of my mother's body against mine.

At the All-Night Laundromat

She stomped in, tracking rock salt and snow,
hacking so loudly into her gnarled hand
the lake-wind stopped wailing a moment
to listen. Cursing, she hefted the trash bag
from her shoulder, undid the frayed rope
and laid out the bodies of rag dolls, wiping
their eyeless, mouthless faces as white ticking
spilled from the stitching where she'd
tried to fix them. In that jaundiced light,
she placed each one in the dryer and watched
them tumble, flailing, limbs crumpled
against the round window. She put her hand
on the shuddering machine the way a mother
presses her palm against a humming incubator
and, falling to her knees, mumbled, *Please,
please,* caressing the warm glass.

In a Blizzard

The night was alive with falling snow—
white hiding the dome of the Capitol
until, from a distance, it looked like
one of those cairns the Inuit used to stack
at each pass, a heap of stones in the shape
of a man they could stop and talk to,
or reach out and touch with stiff hands
when the mountain wind cut close.
As I rounded the frozen river, I saw it
on the fresh snow—a cigarette, not yet wet
or ruined. And though I'd quit years ago,
I picked it up, slipped it in my pocket
and ducked into a diner where I asked
for matches and a cup of steaming coffee.
Almost home, I held that hot Styrofoam
up to the plow now grinding along my street,
toasting the unseen man spreading rock salt
like alms, bringing some noise to the rows
of tucked-in houses his yellow lights
kept caressing. I stepped onto my porch,
struck a match and lit the cigarette,
letting the smoke bloom in the bitter air
where it hovered for an instant
as if it couldn't bear to leave.

Visitation on Telegraph Road

My dead father came back to me
the night I wrecked my pickup.
No gauzy white sheets, no face afloat
in the sleet blowing through
the broken windshield—I just knew
he was there in the seat next to me.
As I slumped over the steering wheel
bleeding onto my jeans, something
tried to fly up out of me and join
the skiff of clouds that hid the moon,
but my father wouldn't let it.
He wrapped what felt like a wool
blanket tight around me so nothing
could escape but the labored
puffs of my own white breath.
No pain rose yet from cracked ribs
or the gash in my head as the thread
in me that had almost snapped
held taut beneath my father's touch.
When a rush of wind shook the truck,
I took out my phone, but the numbers
were unreadable until that blanket
lifted from me with a shudder
and grazed the side of my face
rough as the rubbing kiss of stubble.
I dialed 911, felt the seat, but knew
as soon as I heard that ringing, I was
back in the world, and he was not.

Visitation on a Red Line Train

And being dead is hard work and full of retrieval . . .
—Rainer Maria Rilke

This man who could be my father circa 1975,
with his salt-and-pepper mustache and tight T-shirt,
boards the train at Downtown Crossing,

brushing off his hoodie before pressing himself
into the crush of drenched bodies. No surprise
he's come back to me now in the form of a stranger

I'm already in love with as he digs through a knapsack
crammed with paintbrushes and tubes of pigment,
pulling out a swollen, rain-ruined copy of Rilke's

Duino Elegies, and then holding tight to the tether
of every word as the train lurches to life again.
Why wouldn't my father choose to assume

the body of the boy he once was, drawing a smoke
from the pack in his pocket and placing it behind
an ear I know is crosshatched with faint white scars

from home-haircuts his father had insisted
on giving him while drunk. But now he's elbowing
through the crowd as we screech into a tunnel

and stop. The doors open, and he's out before
I can scrawl my number on the steamed-over window.
His hood up, he tosses back one last glance, lets

the unlit cigarette hang from his lips as he passes
through the turnstile, steps onto the escalator
and is slowly lifted into the station above.

I Consider Again Our Transience

What do you think death will be like?
I ask my friend at the busy Whole Foods
where we sit, eating overpriced salads,
the flaps of our cardboard containers
opened like wings about to take flight.
She tells me she thinks it'll be like
switching off the lights—first we were
nowhere, then here, and then we'll be
nowhere again for a while. She spears
a piece of asparagus with her plastic fork,
brings it to her lips and pauses. *And you?*
I say I'm not sure, but I've always thought
death would be a kind of waiting room
where we'll have to sit for long stretches
wondering what'll happen next to us,
which is to say it will be a lot like life,
with less noise perhaps. *Makes all this
seem pretty silly*, she points at the salad bar
and checkouts. *Us too*, I say, tapping this
table by the window where we slowly
finish our lunches, leaf by soggy leaf.

My Father in the Rustling Trees

I pick the lock of every knock in the night
or rasp of leaves until I hear his voice as it was
in life. Even when I want the past as charred
as heartwood turned to cinder no hand can make
whole again, I say a grace for the cold scraps
memory serves, and I feel his lips pressed
to my forehead, testing for fever, then a palm
rubbing salve on my chest so when I breathe
I breathe heat, only the bedsprings wheezing
as he rises slow as smoke and switches off
the lights. His soft *Sweet dreams* sending me
into a sleep that would last and last until
the day I saw snow in his eyes, and he said
Don't be sad, and then I wasn't, I was
already listening to the trees.

Sungrazer

Neighbors down the street have strung
chandeliers from the branches
of sycamores in their front yard,
and as I walk by trees with every leaf lit—
their whole house a beacon—I think
of the ISON comet, scheduled to cruise
by Earth tonight, and called a *sungrazer*
for how close it will come to our star.
It has been barreling toward us
for over a million years, having traveled
from the Oort Cloud on the outskirts
of the solar system where leftover debris
of planetesimals spins in a sphere
as if waiting to be of use again.
Made mostly of ice and dust, the comet,
once it nears the sun, will boomerang back
much brighter—still alive—or will
turn to haze, boiled away by heat.
If it does survive, it will appear
in the sky after midnight—a ball of light
shooting past us, leaving a trail
we can trace with our naked eyes.

The Body Electric

Every cell in our bodies contains a pore
like a door, which says when to let in
the flood of salt-ions bearing their charge,
but the power in us moves much slower
than the current that rushes into wires
to ignite the lamp by which I undress,
am told to undress by sparks that cross
the gap of a synapse to pass along
the message, *It's time for sleep*. As I pull
back the sheets, ease into bed, I think
if I could only look beneath my skin,
I'd see my body as alive as Hong Kong,
veins of night traffic crawling along
the freeways as tiny faces inside taxis
look up from the glow of their phones,
sensing that someone is watching.

Elegy for TV Snow

I fell asleep during the apocalypse tonight—
yet another late movie about a man out to save
his estranged family from the rapture of rising
floodwaters, crumbling floors, toppling
skyscrapers—the destruction of the earth,
I'm ashamed to admit, like a lullaby to me.
But when I wake today, here's morning
pushing its cold breath through windows
I've left open, a palpable mist guarding
the mountains that have not swallowed
our small town overnight. As the muted TV
spreads its blue glow throughout the room,
I suddenly miss that snowy analog static
whose fazed-out crackle always eased me
into dreams when not even Valium could
bring on the blessings of sleep. I find myself
still longing for those fossilized signals
sent out just after the Big Bang, white noise
of worlds being made and unmade.

Before Language

If you had stumbled on
a band of feral humans
in the days before language
you would have heard nothing
but the snapping of twigs
underfoot as they moved
across moss and leaves
to drink from the creek
and pick salmonberries
whose sweet, pink crush
between their teeth was
the only speech they needed.
Like the animals, we too
once spoke using mostly
gesture—a turn of the head,
a flex of the haunches
or flick of the ears that said
something quick was coming
to end our noble silence.

On a Hike

The feeding elk flinched, flustered
by my sudden presence on the trail,
and then I saw the whole herd browsing
patches of wood sorrel near the firs.
As I stood there, unmoving, they all
paused in mid-chew, strands of grass
and leaves hanging from their mouths
as they watched to see if what I held
was more than just a fallen branch.
Rifle was not a word they needed to know:
they recognized that shape, recalled
the shattering report of every shot
that had torn through the skin of silence
stretched tight around this mountain.
I wanted to lie down between them,
show them I had come here in peace,
but they knew better: though they made
no sound, a ripple of decision soon
passed among them, and they began
to move as one back up the ridge,
heavy hooves loosing clumps of loam
as they blazed a trail away from me.

Message

I wanted to capture that quiet moment
after the heron splashed up from the pond,
when a pair of wings opened wide in me
and white space erased every thought I had.
I could hear bullfrogs beginning to thrum
their mud-songs, could feel the blue blades
of fescue lying down for the coming storm,
but the chirping of the phone in my pocket
broke the calm, and before the heron could
turn to a gray speck among stacked clouds,
I was thinking again, wondering who it was,
then taking out the phone, tapping its screen
aglow with the image of a yellow envelope
waiting to be opened, my moment of stillness
floating off with tufts of thistledown caught
on the wind of the world's wild mind.

Coyote

This body will never be a field of fescue
and bluestem meant for grazing,
but I'm a glutton for the sun,
clinging to the only light that holds me,
craving rain one minute, and fire the next—
that black rebirth. We want to be fed
and, once sated, wait for death circling
above us like a hawk-shadow,
wanting to be lifted out of our weakness.
Is that all there is? Now that I live alone,
and my hapless inner yapping
at every hangdog moon looking down on me
has stopped, I too have stopped begging
for a scrap of dream to climb into bed with me.
I can lie back in this patch of clover
next to my hunger. No watch, no phone,
no whisper in my ear warm with want—
I want only the wind today
drying my sweat to salt-film, bearing
whiffs of me to the den under the ridge
where the coyote, no longer dozing,
smacks his lips, licks the tips of his canines,
his eyes aflame with so much meat
suddenly within reach. But as the smile
fades from his face, he rests his head again
on folded paws, knowing the greater pleasure
is often the fantasy that spares
the shirtless man lying prone in the grass.

On the Water

I was jealous of the two men sitting next to me
on the deck of that restaurant in Malibu
overlooking the Pacific. Their glasses of sangria
shone in the glow of overhead lanterns,
and they held hands, fingers interlaced as they
scanned the rumpled gray sheet of ocean
for a trace of promised dolphins or whales.
But when none appeared, and the marine layer
began to creep inland, the men rose together
and rubbed each other's arms before carrying
their half-drunk drinks and plates of calamari
to a candlelit table inside. Then I was alone
in the June gloom, standing at the edge
of the deck where I watched until the silver
fins of a pod of dolphins sliced through
the choppy water, each of them leaping
with relief into the now cooler air
no one else was breathing.

Nostalgia

Boys outside are playing basketball,
and every time I hear the smack
of rubber on asphalt, I feel our bodies—
that damp slap again of skin on skin.
But there is a fine line between fantasy
and honest desire, a difference between
drapes dancing in a phantom breeze
and the ghost in me who still remembers
kissing the veins snaking up your biceps.
I lie here by the open window, waiting
for the low flame under the pot of rice
to do its work, waiting for each grain
to absorb the water and soften.
The kale's been massaged with lemon
and the tofu fried the way you like it.
The boys have hauled their voices inside,
but the birds won't stop singing until
the sun stops bleeding into the sky above
the line of pines, which grow more
fragrant and restless tonight as they rub
against each other in the resin-scented
wind at twilight.

Note to Self

Leave the TV off tonight and put
your phone on silent. Pour the wine
in your glass down the drain.
Taste the homemade raspberry jam
friends sent packed in a box
with balled-up newspaper so the jar
wouldn't break on its way to you.
Treat each fragile moment like that
and make of this instant something
sweet to smear on toasted bread,
then feast alone while standing
and staring out at the bare magnolia.

When the World Is Taken from Me

I know I will miss that first messy bite
into an apple, burst of late summer
light on the tongue, dripping from my lips.
And forcing open the window that sticks,
pushing up, feeling it give inch by inch
until there's air. And hearing my own name
called out on a crowded train, knowing
that one familiar face in the crush of faces.
We see the world best when we remember
what might disappear: Thinking of the bees,
I eat half a jar of raw honey, amber-gold
as an autumn sunset. I call my mother,
and we talk about the weather, whether
or not the frost will kill her four o'clocks.

The Question

Haloed by the glow of machines
in his last room at the ICU,
my father smiled like a child and asked
in his old voice: *How do you know
I'm always with you?* as if he were
already gone. And as he settled back
into a stack of pillows, I told him:
That faint pressure on the nape of my neck
before sleep. Streetlights that blink
on and off as I pass beneath.
The urge to turn and look behind me.
Words that come out of nowhere.
The man who said *Evening* to me at the park
last night, blue eyes like cut glass
as bright as yours in the coming dark.

But how do you know? he asked again,
still unconvinced. I listened to the buzz
of fluorescent lights above us,
the squeak of a nurse's shoes as she
bustled by the room, but my mind was now
as blank as the space on the wall
behind his bed. My father then
laced his fingers together and placed
both hands in his lap as if
he had all the time in the world
to wait for my answer.

Acknowledgments

I'd like to thank the editors of the following publications in which versions of these poems appeared or were reprinted, sometimes in slightly different form: *American Life in Poetry*, *Blue River*, *The Cape Rock*, *Cascadia Review*, *Fourth River*, *The Huffington Post*, *Hunger Mountain*, *Linebreak*, *The New Republic*, *North American Review*, *The North Coast Journal*, *Ploughshares*, *Poet Lore*, *Poetry East*, *Raleigh Review*, *Ruminate Magazine*, *Slipstream*, *Southern Poetry Review*, *Split Rock Review*, *Verse Daily*, and *Verse-Virtual*.

A selection of these poems also appeared as *How Light Leaves*, a chapbook published by FutureCycle Press in 2016. Many thanks to the staff at FutureCycle, especially Diane Kistner, who offered kind and invaluable editorial advice, which made this a much better book.

Boundless gratitude to the Dorothy Sargent Rosenberg Foundation for prizes in 2012 and 2014, and to the English Department at the University of Nebraska-Lincoln for its Othmer Fellowship and years of support that allowed me to work on this book free from financial worry. Poems in this collection were also completed at several artist residencies, including Kimmel Harding Nelson Center for the Arts, Caldera Arts, and Sitka Center for the Arts. For reading through the manuscript at various stages and offering advice and direction, I thank my wonderful friends and teachers: David Axelrod, Grace Bauer, David Clewell, Kim Hays, Ted Kooser, Travis Mossotti, and Stella Nelson. Gratitude to Sarah Chavez, Eileen Durgin-Clinchard, Pat Emile, Clarence Harlon-Orsi, Robert Lipscomb, and Nick White for making Nebraska feel like home. Thanks also to Shari Stenberg for dharma talks that continue to center and inspire me.

Many friends also provided space in their homes for me while I was completing this book: Special thanks to Adrienne Knowles and Luca Eandi; Cole and Billy Helmkamp; Kim Hays and Amanda Noska; Tracy Swigert; Stella Nelson and Axel Steuerwald; Fran and Howard Kaye; Trey and Jennifer Moody; Heather Swan; and Jesse Lee Kercheval and Dan Fuller.

I would like to thank my wonderful students in the Eastern Oregon

University MFA program for constant inspiration, and my colleagues, especially David Axelrod, Jennifer Boyden, Justin Hocking, Megan Kruse, and Jodi Varon, for giving me a second home in the West.

Words cannot express my gratitude to Dr. Susan Swartwout for choosing this manuscript for the Vern Cowles Prize, and for all of her support over the years. I'd also like to thank the staff at Southeast Missouri State University Press, including Carrie Walker and Dr. James Brubaker, for producing such a beautiful book, as well as Dixon Hearne for his ongoing support of the Cowles Prize.

Lastly, this book is for my father, but it was also written with the support of my mother, Cindy Crews, my brother, Ron Crews, and my husband, Brad Peacock, who reminds me every day to lead with love.

Printed and bound by PG in the USA